Handy Tennessee Genealogy Handbook

By Gary L. Morris

©2015 Gary L. Morris

ISBN-13: 978-1507658857

ISBN-10: 1507658850

Table of Contents

Notes

Genealogical Research in Tennessee

Because of its long and colorful history, there are many historical and genealogical records and resources available for tracing your family history in Tennessee. Because of the abundance of information held at many different locations, tracking down the records for your ancestor can be an ominous task. Don't worry though, we know just where they are, and we'll show you which records you'll need, while helping you to understand:

1. What they are
2. Where to find them
3. How to use them

These records can be found both online and off, so we'll introduce you to online websites, indexes and databases, as well as brick-and-mortar repositories and other institutions that will help with your research in Tennessee. So that you will have a more comprehensive understanding of these records, we have provided a brief history of the "Volunteer State" to illustrate what type of records may have been generated during specific time periods. That information will assist you in pinpointing times and locations on which to focus the search for your Tennessee ancestors and their records.

A Brief History of Tennessee

The Yuchi and Creek Indians were living in the area that is now East Tennessee when the first Europeans arrived in the early 1500's. They would be joined by the Cherokee about 200 years later, a powerful tribe that would eventually dominate the area until they were forced out by the federal government in the 1830's. The western part of the state was inhabited by the Chicksaw, while the Shawnee occupied the Cumberland Valley area until being driven out by the Chickasaw and Cherokee.

European traders and explorers traversed the area for over two hundred years before any permanent settlements were established, searching the area for furs, pelts, and anything else they could find. The most famous of these early explorers was Daniel Boone, who lived in the area that is now Washington County. At the end of the French and Indian War in 1763, many from Virginia and North Carolina crossed the Allegheny Mountains into the region, and by 1770 small white settlements began to develop in the area between the Cumberland and Unaka Mountains known as the Cumberland Basin.

A second area of development was in the northeast along the Nolichucky, Holston, and Watauga Rivers. The settlements in this area would merge to create the Watauga Association in 1771. In the Cumberland basin area, a gentleman by the name of James Robertson would, in 1779, establish a town called Nashborough which would one day be known as Nashville.

The Revolutionary War did not reach Tennessee, but many of the frontiersmen fought in Virginia and the Carolinas. The Revolution was hardly over when Tennesseans began to seek statehood for themselves. The area remained part of North Carolina until 1790 when North Carolina ceded the area to the United States. At that time Tennessee became known as the Southwest territory. A capitol was establishes at Knoxville, and steps were taken to secure statehood which was granted on June 1, 1796.

In the period between statehood and the Civil War, towns like Knoxville, Nashville, and other early settlements became flourishing frontier towns. The state was divided over slavery, most slaveholders living in the western part of the state where cotton was grown. In this part of the state blacks made up nearly one quarter of the population, while in the east, only around on tenth of the populace was black. Emancipation was considered at the constitutional convention in 1834, but it was decided to keep slavery in place.

West Tennessee was purchased from the Chickasaw, and it was here that the cotton industry took off. Memphis was established in 1821, and soon became the states principal marketing center for cotton. Tobacco flourished in the counties of the Highland Rim, and Tennessee soon became the nation's third largest producer of tobacco behind Kentucky and Virginia. Most Tennesseans were in favor of secession when the Civil War approached, by those in the east remained staunchly loyal to the Union, and many fled to Kentucky to join the union army.

Tennessee was a major battleground during the war; some of the bloodiest battles of the encounter took place at Chattanooga in the Battle of Chickamauga, while the final defeat of Confederate General John B. Hood's forces at Nashville and Franklin were the last clashes on Tennessee soil. Tennessee was readmitted to the union following the Civil war, and was actually the only former Confederate state not to be ruled by a military government. Economic recovery was faster than in other areas of the South, and by the 1890's paper, flour, and cotton mills were flourishing, as Memphis became the nation's leading producer of cottonseed oil.

Important Dates in Tennessee History

1663 – Part of French territory

1763 – Area ceded by France to Great Britain

1771 – Watagua Valley Association formed

1776 – Becomes Washington County, Tennessee

1779 – Nashville founded

1780 – Battle of King's Mountain

1784 – Ceded from North Carolina to the United States

1789 – Placed under the jurisdiction of North Carolina

1790 – Area ceded back to the United States

1796 – Statehood

1861 – Secedes from Union

1866 – Readmitted to Union

Famous Battles Fought in Tennessee

Although the Revolutionary War **Battle of King's Mountain** was fought in North Carolina, many Tennessee volunteers and patriots fought in the clash. There were close to 40 clashes between Union and Confederate troops during the Civil war, the **Tennessee GenWeb Project** has a listing and related facts for all Civil War Battles fought on Tennessee soil.

Battle of King's Mountain: http://www.britishbattles.com/kings-mountain.htm

Tennessee GenWeb Project:
http://www.tngenweb.org/civilwar/misc/battles.html

The battle accounts that exist can be very effective in uncovering the military records of your ancestor. They can tell you what regiments fought in which battles, and often include the names and ranks of many officers and enlisted men.

Common Tennessee Genealogical Issues and Resources to Overcome Them

Boundary Changes: Boundary changes are a common obstacle when researching Tennessee ancestors. You could be searching for an ancestor's record in one county when in fact it is stored in a different one due to historical county boundary changes.

The **Atlas of Historical County Boundaries** can help you to overcome that problem. It provides a chronological listing of every boundary change that has occurred in the history of Tennessee.

Atlas of Historical County Boundaries:
http://publications.newberry.org/ahcbp/documents/TN_Consolidated _Chronology.htm#Consolidated_Chronology

Name Changes: Surname changes, variations, and misspellings can complicate genealogical research. It is important to check all spelling variations. Soundex, a program that indexes names by sound, is a useful first step, but you can't rely on it completely as some name variations result in different Soundex codes. The surnames could be different, but the first name may be different too. You can also find records filed under initials, middle names, and nicknames as well, so you will need to **get creative with surname variations** and spellings in order to cover all the possibilities. For help with surname variations read our instructional article on **How to Use Soundex**.

get creative with surname variations:
http://obituarieshelp.org/blog/?p=634

How to Use Soundex: http://obituarieshelp.org/blog/?p=505

Tennessee Genealogical Organizations and Archives

Genealogical resources include not only records, but the organizations that house them, or can direct you to them. These institutions include: *Archives, Libraries, Genealogical Societies, Family History Centers, Universities, Churches, and Museums.*

Following are links to their websites, their physical addresses, and a summary of the records you can find there.

Archives and Libraries

Tennessee State Library and Archives – African American records, Bibliographies, Vital records, Census records, Historical newspapers, Military records, County Wills and Probate records, historical maps and photographs, Native American records and resources, Manuscripts and City directories

403 7th Avenue North
Nashville, TN 37243
Tel: 615-741-2764
Email: reference.tsla@tn.gov

Tennessee State Library and Archives:
http://www.tn.gov/tsla/Collections.htm

Nashville Public Library - Obituary Index from the Tennessean 1964-2002, Marriages Recorded in Nashville, 1864-1905. Historical photograph collection

615 Church Street
Nashville, TN 37219
Tel: 615-862-5800

Nashville Public Library:
http://www.library.nashville.org/research/res_databases.asp#genealogy

Metro Archives of Nashville and Davidson County – Vital records, Wills, Court records

Metro Archives
3801 Green Hills Village Drive
Nashville, TN 37215
Phone: 615-862-5880
Email: info@nashvillearchives.org

Metro Archives of Nashville and Davidson County:
http://www.nashvillearchives.org/

Memphis and Shelby County Public Library and Information Center - Freedmen's Bureau Marriage Index (1864-1865), and the Memphis/Shelby County Death Index (1848-1945), Civil War Collection, family research indexes, source book published family histories, county records in print and on microfilm, magazines, manuscript holdings, and microfilm of United States census records for 1790 to 1930.

Genealogy Collection
4th Floor, History Department
Benjamin I. Hooks Central Library
3030 Poplar Avenue
Memphis, TN 38111 Tel: 901:415-2700

Memphis and Shelby County Public Library and Information Center: http://www.memphislibrary.org/mplic-home

Vanderbilt University, Jean and Alexander Heard Library – Large manuscript collection including letters, journals, publications, writings, and business papers, rare books, historical photograph collection

419 21st Ave. South
Nashville, TN 37240-0007
Tel: 615-322-7100

Vanderbilt University, Jean and Alexander Heard Library:
http://www.memphislibrary.org/mplic-home

University of Tennessee Knoxville – Civil war collection includes images and military documents – such as muster rolls, generals' orders, and supply requests –also houses a significant amount of correspondence and journals from the era.

Special Collections Library
121 John C. Hodges Library
1015 Volunteer Boulevard
Knoxville, TN 37996
Phone: (865) 974-4480
Email: special@utk.edu

University of Tennessee Knoxville: http://www.lib.utk.edu/special/

The Knox County Archives - Knox County Marriage Licenses and Bonds/Applications, Knox County Divorce Records, Knox County Register of Deeds, Warranty Deed Books, Knox County Probate Records (Wills and Estate Settlements)

East Tennessee History Center
601 S. Gay Street
Knoxville, TN 37902
Phone:
(865) 215-8800
archives@knoxlib.org

The Knox County Archives:
http://knoxrooms.sirsi.net/rooms/portal/page/21590_Knox_County_
Archives

Genealogical and Historical Societies

Genealogical and historical societies have access to extensive catalogues of genealogical data. They are also able to offer expert guidance for genealogical researchers. Many members are professional genealogists who are most willing to share their expertise in finding ancestors.

Tennessee Historical Society - Tennessee Historical Quarterly, Civil War resources

War Memorial Building
300 Capital Blvd.
Nashville, TN 37243
Tel: 615.741.8934
Fax: 615.741.8937
Email: info@tennesseehistory.org

Tennessee Historical Society: http://www.tennesseehistory.org/

Tennessee Genealogical Society – Large Genealogical library and a wealth of resources for researching Tennessee ancestors

7779 Poplar Pike
Germantown
TN 38138-5952

Tennessee Genealogical Society: http://www.tngs.org/

Tennessee Mailing Lists

Mailing lists are internet based facilities that use email to distribute a single message to all who subscribe to it. When information on a particular surname, new records, or any other important genealogy information related to the mailing list topic becomes available, the subscribers are alerted to it. Joining a mailing list is an excellent way to stay up to date on Tennessee genealogy research topics. Rootsweb have an extensive listing of **Tennessee Mailing Lists** on a variety of topics.

Tennessee Mailing Lists:
http://lists.rootsweb.ancestry.com/index/usa/TN/misc.html

Tennessee Message Boards

A message board is another internet based facility where people can post questions about a specific genealogy topic and have it answered by other genealogists. If you have questions about a surname, record type, or research topic, you can post your question and other researchers and genealogists will help you with the answer. Be sure to check back regularly, as the answers are not emailed to you. The Tennessee message boards at **Rootsweb** are completely free to use.

Rootsweb:
http://boards.rootsweb.com/localities.northam.usa.states/mb.ashx

Tennessee Newspapers and Periodicals

Many genealogy periodicals and historical newspapers contain reprinted copies of family genealogies, transcripts of family Bible records, information about local records and archives, census indexes, church records, queries, land records, obituaries, court records, cemetery records, and wills. The following sites have historical Tennessee newspapers and periodicals that you can search online or on-site.

Tennessee State Library and Archives - Collection includes almost every existent newspaper published in Tennessee.

403 7th Avenue North
Nashville, TN 37243
Tel: 615-741-2764
Email: reference.tsla@tn.gov

Tennessee State Library and Archives:
http://www.tn.gov/tsla/Collections.htm

Williamson County Public Library - Williamson County newspapers from the 1821 to date

1314 Columbia Ave.
Franklin, TN 37064
Telephone: 615-794-3105
Fax: 615-595-1245

Williamson County Public Library: http://lib.williamson-tn.org/

GenealogyBank.com – free searchable database of Tennessee newspaper archives, 1793-1969

GenealogyBank.com:
http://www.genealogybank.com/gbnk/newspapers/explore/USA/Tennessee/

The Online Books Page – links to historical Tennessee books and periodicals available for viewing online

The Online Books Page:
http://onlinebooks.library.upenn.edu/webbin/book/browse?type=subject&c=c&key=tennessee

Library of Congress Digital Newspaper Directory – free searchable database of historical U.S. newspapers dating from 1690-present

Library of Congress Digital Newspaper Directory:
http://chroniclingamerica.loc.gov/search/titles/

NewspaperArchive.com – largest online database of historical newspapers in the world.

NewspaperArchive.com: http://newspaperarchive.com/

Historical Tennessee Maps and Gazetteers

Maps are an integral part of genealogical research. They help us to locate landmarks, towns, cities, parishes, states, provinces, waterways and roads and streets. They also help us to determine when and where boundary changes might have taken place, and give us a visualization of the area we're researching in.

For locating place names, a gazetteer is the best possible resource for any genealogist. Gazetteers are also sometimes called "place name dictionaries", and can help you to locate the area in which you need to conduct research. Below are links to the maps and gazetteers for research in Tennessee.

Peabody GNIS Service – Tennessee:
http://peabody.research.yale.edu/cgi-bin/Query.GNIS?ST=Tennessee&SU=1

Color Landform Atlas – Tennessee:
http://fermi.jhuapl.edu/states/tn_0.html

1985 U.S. Atlas: http://www.livgenmi.com/1895/TN/

Tennessee Hometown Locator:
http://tennessee.hometownlocator.com/

Tennessee City Directories

.

City directories are similar to telephone directories in that they list the residents of a particular area. The difference though is what is important to genealogists, and that is they pre-date telephone directories. You can find an ancestor's information such as their street address, place of employment, occupation, or the name of their spouse. A one-stop-shop for finding city directories in Tennessee is the **Tennessee Online Historical Directories** which contains a listing of every available online historical directory related to Tennessee. Another useful site is **US City Directories** which identifies printed, microfilmed, and online Tennessee directories and their repositories.

Tennessee Online Historical Directories:
https://sites.google.com/site/onlinedirectorysite/Home/usa/tn

US City Directories: http://www.uscitydirectories.com/sd.htm

Tennessee State Library and Archives – Huge collection of Tennessee city directories dating from mid-nineteenth century

403 7th Avenue North
Nashville, TN 37243
Tel: 615-741-2764
Email: reference.tsla@tn.gov

Tennessee State Library and Archives:
http://www.tn.gov/tsla/Collections.htm

Tennessee Genealogical Records

Birth, Death, Marriage and Divorce Records – Also known as vital records, birth, death, and marriage certificates are the most basic, yet most important records attached to your ancestor. The reason for their importance is that they not only place your ancestor in a specific place at a definite time, but potentially connect the individual to other relatives. Below is a list of repositories and websites where you can find Tennessee vital records.

Tennessee Vital Records - The Tennessee Vital Records Office keeps birth records for 100 years and death, marriage, and divorce records for 50 years; after that time, the records are sent to the Tennessee State Library and Archives for public access and family research.

1st Floor, Central Services Building
421 Fifth Avenue, North
Nashville, TN 37243
615-741-1763
1-855-809-0072

Tennessee Vital Records: http://health.state.tn.us/Vr/index.htm

Tennessee State Library and Archives - Burial Records of Federal Soldiers by W.R. Cornelius and Company, Davidson County Death Records 1900-1913, Death Notices in Nashville Newspapers 1855-1907, Index to Tennessee Death Records 1908-1912, Nashville Obituaries & Death Notices for 1913, Statewide Index to Tennessee Death Records (1914 - 1933)

403 7th Avenue North
Nashville, TN 37243
Tel: 615-741-2764
Email: reference.tsla@tn.gov

Tennessee State Library and Archives:
http://www.tn.gov/tsla/Collections.htm

Nashville Public Library - Marriages Recorded in Nashville, 1864-1905

615 Church Street
Nashville, TN 37219
Tel: 615-862-5800

Nashville Public Library:
http://www.library.nashville.org/research/res_databases.asp#genealogy

Williamson County Public Library - specializes in Williamson County, Tennessee genealogy, African American genealogy, local authors, local history, and Civil War materials, and includes genealogy materials for surrounding counties, the State of Tennessee, and surrounding states.

1314 Columbia Ave.
Franklin, TN 37064
Telephone: 615-794-3105
Fax: 615-595-1245

Williamson County Public Library: http://lib.williamson-tn.org/

Memphis and Shelby County Public Library and Information Center - Freedmen's Bureau Marriage Index (1864-1865), and the Memphis/Shelby County Death Index (1848-1945)

Genealogy Collection
4th Floor, History Department
Benjamin I. Hooks Central Library
3030 Poplar Avenue
Memphis, TN 38111 Tel: 901:415-2700

Memphis and Shelby County Public Library and Information Center: http://www.memphislibrary.org/mplic-home

Metro Archives of Nashville and Davidson County – Nashville Birth Records 1881-1913, Davidson County Birth Record Index 1908-1912, Death Records 1874-1904, Marriages 1788-1830, Marriages 1905-1916, Nashville Marriages 1864-1905

Metro Archives
3801 Green Hills Village Drive
Nashville, TN 37215
Phone: 615-862-5880
Email: info@nashvillearchives.org

Metro Archives of Nashville and Davidson County:
http://www.nashvillearchives.org/

The Knox County Archives - Marriage records 1792–1974, Knoxville birth and death records, 1881–1911

East Tennessee History Center
601 S. Gay Street
Knoxville, TN 37902
Phone:
(865) 215-8800
archives@knoxlib.org

The Knox County Archives:
http://knoxrooms.sirsi.net/rooms/portal/page/21590_Knox_County_Archives

Family Search has the following indexes that can be searched online for free:

Tennessee, Births and Christenings, 1828-1939:
https://familysearch.org/search/collection/1681012

Tennessee, County Marriages, 1790-1950:
https://familysearch.org/search/collection/1619127

Tennessee, Death Records, 1914-1955:
https://familysearch.org/search/collection/1417505

Tennessee, Deaths and Burials, 1874-1955:
https://familysearch.org/search/collection/1681020

Tennessee, Marriages, 1796-1950:
https://familysearch.org/search/collection/1681022

Tennessee, Putnam County Marriages, 1930-1961:
https://familysearch.org/search/collection/1877098

Tennessee, State Marriage Index, 1780-2002:
https://familysearch.org/search/collection/1936414

Census Records

Census records are among the most important genealogical documents for placing your ancestor in a particular place at a specific time. Like BDM records, they can also lead you to other ancestors, particularly those who were living under the authority of the head of household.

Tennessee State Library and Archives - 1810 Census for Grainger County and Rutherford County, 1820 (most of the records for counties in east Tennessee are missing), 1830 - 1880 (complete), 1900 - 1930 (complete). The 1830-1930 records can also be vewed online at the State Archives website.

403 7th Avenue North
Nashville, TN 37243
Tel: 615-741-2764
Email: reference.tsla@tn.gov

Tennessee State Library and Archives:
http://www.tn.gov/tsla/Collections.htm

Memphis and Shelby County Public Library and Information Center - United States census records for 1790 to 1930.

Genealogy Collection
4th Floor, History Department
Benjamin I. Hooks Central Library
3030 Poplar Avenue
Memphis, TN 38111 Tel: 901:415-2700

Memphis and Shelby County Public Library and Information Center: http://www.memphislibrary.org/mplic-home

The **Free Census Project** has transcribed many Tennessee indexes and new material is added daily

Free Census Project: http://usgwcensus.org/cenfiles/tn.htm

Access Genealogy – Tennessee county census records dating from 1850

Access Genealogy:
http://www.accessgenealogy.com/census/tennessee-census-records.htm

African American Census Schedules Online – slave schedules, mortality schedules, slave-owners census

African American Census Schedules Online:
http://www.afrigeneas.com/aacensus/ga/

Native Americans in Census Records (US National Archives):
http://www.archives.gov/research/census/native-americans/

Tennessee Church Records

Church and synagogue records are a valuable resource, especially for baptisms, marriages, and burials that took place before 1900. You will need to at least have an idea of your ancestor's religious denomination, and in most cases you will have to visit a brick and mortar establishment to view them.

Most church records are kept by the individual church, although in some denominations, records are placed in a regional archive or maintained at the diocesan level. Local Historical Societies are sometimes the repository for the state's older church records. Below are links archives that maintain church records, as well as a few databases that can be viewed online.

The **Family History Library** contains many church records from a variety of denominations on microfilm.

Family History Library:
http://familysearch.org/learn/wiki/en/Family_History_Library

Central Repositories for Denominational Records

Church of Jesus Christ of Latter-day Saints (Mormons)

Early Mormon Church records for Tennessee can be found on film located at the LDS Family History Library in Salt Lake City and can be searched via the **Family History Library Catalog**

Family History Library Catalog:
https://familysearch.org/eng/Library/FHLC/frameset_fhlc.asp

Disciples of Christ

Disciples of Christ Historical Society
1101 Nineteenth Avenue South
Nashville, TN 37212-2196
Telephone: 1-866-834-7563 (toll free)

Disciples of Christ Historical Society:
http://www.discipleshistory.org/

Lutheran

James R. Crumley, Jr. Archives
Lutheran Theological Southern Seminary
4201 North Main Street
Columbia, SC 29203
Telephone: 803-786-5150 x234
E-mail: archives@ltss.edu

James R. Crumley, Jr. Archives: http://crumleyarchives.org/

Methodist

Three Methodist conferences oversee the missions and business of the church in Tennessee. The conferences house records from churches that have closed; records of existing congregations are generally still in the churches. The Holston Conference oversees the eastern third of the state, the Tennessee Conference oversees the middle third, and the Memphis Conference oversees the western third.

Holston Conference
Office:
P.O. Box 850
Alcoa, TN 37701
Telephone: 1-866-690-4080
Fax: 1-865-690-3162

The archives of the Holston Conference of the United Methodist Church are housed at the Kelly Library of Emory and Henry College.

Kelly Library
Emory and Henry College
P.O. Box 948
30480 Ambrister Drive
Emory VA 24327
Telephone: 1-540-944-6668

Kelly Library: http://www.ehc.edu/academics/resources/kelly-library

Tennessee Conference
520 Commerce Street, Suite 205
Nashville, TN 37203
Telephone: 1-615-263-0518 (call to make an appointment)

Tennessee Conference: http://www.tnumc.org/

Memphis Conference United Methodist Archives
Luther L. Gobbel Library
Lambuth University
705 Lambuth Boulevard
Jackson, TN 38301
Telephone: 1-901-425-3270

Memphis Conference United Methodist Archives:
http://www.memphis.edu/lambuth/library.php

Presbyterian

Presbyterian Historical Society
425 Lombard Street
Philadelphia, PA 19147
Telephone: 1-215-627-1852
Fax: 1-215-627-0509

Presbyterian Historical Society http://www.history.pcusa.org/

Roman Catholic

Diocese of Knoxville
805 Northshore Drive Southwest
Knoxville, TN 37919
Telephone: 865-584-3307
Fax: 865-584-7538

Diocese of Knoxville: http://www.dioknox.org/

Diocese of Nashville
The Catholic Center
2400 Twenty-first Avenue, South
Nashville, TN 37212-5387
Telephone: 1-615-383-6393
Fax: 1-615-292-8411

Diocese of Nashville: http://www.dioceseofnashville.com/

Diocese of Memphis
The Catholic Center
5825 Shelby Oaks Drive
Memphis, TN 38134-7316
Telephone: 1-901-373-1200
Fax: 1-901-373-1269

Diocese of Memphis: http://www.cdom.org/

Tennessee Military Records

More than 40 million Americans have participated in some kind of war service since America was colonized. The chance of finding your ancestor amongst those records is exceptionally high. Military records can even reveal individuals who never actually served, such as those who registered for the two World Wars but were never called to duty.

Below are a number of links to websites and archives that contain Tennessee military records.

Tennessee State Library and Archives - War of 1812, Civil War, Spanish American War, World War I, Korean War, and Vietnam War records of Tennessee soldiers

403 7th Avenue North
Nashville, TN 37243
Tel: 615-741-2764
Email: reference.tsla@tn.gov

Tennessee State Library and Archives:
http://www.tn.gov/tsla/Collections.htm

Williamson County Public Library - Tennessee Confederate pension applications, Tennessee Confederate Widows' pension applications, and service records of soldiers in Williamson County Companies.

1314 Columbia Ave.
Franklin, TN 37064
Telephone: 615-794-3105
Fax: 615-595-1245

Williamson County Public Library: http://lib.williamson-tn.org/

US Department of Veterans Affairs Nationwide Gravesite Locator – includes information on veterans and their family members buried in veterans and military cemeteries having a government grave marker.

US Department of Veterans Affairs Nationwide Gravesite Locator: http://gravelocator.cem.va.gov/

Family Search has the following indexes which are searchable online for free:

Tennessee, Civil War Service Records of Confederate Soldiers, 1861-1865 link to:
https://familysearch.org/search/collection/1932378

Tennessee, Civil War Service Records of Union Soldiers, 1861-1865: https://familysearch.org/search/collection/1932422

Tennessee, Confederate Pension Applications, Soldiers and Widows, 1891-1965:
https://familysearch.org/search/collection/1874474

You may also find your ancestor's military records in the following databases:

United States General Index to Pension Files, 1861-1934

United States General Index to Pension Files, 1861-1934:
https://familysearch.org/search/collection/1919699

United States Index to Service Records, War with Spain, 1898

United States Index to Service Records, War with Spain, 1898 :
https://familysearch.org/search/collection/1919583

United States Index to Indian Wars Pension Files, 1892-1926 – military pension records of soldiers who fought in the Indian Wars between 1817 and 1898

United States Index to Indian Wars Pension Files, 1892-1926: https://familysearch.org/search/collection/1979427

United States Registers of Enlistments in the U.S. Army, 1798-1914 - index of men who enlisted in the United States Army, 1798-1914.

United States Registers of Enlistments in the U.S. Army, 1798-1914: https://familysearch.org/search/collection/1880762

United States Mexican War Pension Index, 1887-1926 - index to Mexican War pension files for service between 1846 and 1848

United States Mexican War Pension Index, 1887-1926: https://familysearch.org/search/collection/1979390

Civil War Soldiers Service Records - Service records for both Union and Confederate soldiers indexed by soldier's name, rank, and unit.

Civil War Soldier Service Records: http://go.fold3.com/civilwar_records/

Tennessee Cemetery Records

As convenient as it is to search cemetery records online, keep in mind that there are a few disadvantages over visiting a cemetery in person. They are:

- Tombstone information is not always accurately transcribed
- The arrangement of the graves in a cemetery can be crucial as family members are often buried next to each other or in the same grave. This arrangement is not always preserved in the alphabetical indexes that are found online.

With that information in mind, the following websites have databases that can be searched online for Tennessee Cemetery records.

Tennessee GenWeb Cemetery Project - contains all cemeteries in the US Geological Survey for Tennessee as well as several cemeteries that are not identified by the USG

Tennessee GenWeb Cemetery Project:
http://www.tngenweb.org/cemeteries/

Tennessee Tombstone Transcription Project - death and burial records

Tennessee Tombstone Transcription Project:
http://www.usgwtombstones.org/tennessee/tenn.html

African American Cemeteries Online – African American, slave, and Native American cemetery records

African American Cemeteries Online:
http://africanamericancemeteries.com/ar/

Access Genealogy – database of Tennessee cemetery record transcriptions

Access Genealogy:
http://www.accessgenealogy.com/cemetery/tennessee-cemetery-records.htm

Find a Grave – over 100 million grave records can be searched on this site. Search can be conducted by name, location, or cemetery name.

Find a Grave: http://www.findagrave.com/

Interment.net - A free online database containing approximately 4 million cemetery records from around the world.

Interment.net: http://www.interment.net/

Billion Graves – as the name implies, you can search a billion records including headstone photos, transcriptions, cemetery records, and grave locations.

Billion Graves:
http://billiongraves.com/pages/search/index.php#cemetery

Tennessee Obituaries

Obituaries can reveal a wealth about our ancestor and other relatives. You can search our **Tennessee Obituaries Listings** from hundreds of Tennessee newspapers online for free.

Tennessee Obituaries Listings:
http://obituarieshelp.org/tennessee_newspaper_obituaries.html

Tennessee Wills and Probate Records

The documents found in a probate packet may include a complete inventory of a person's estate, newspaper entries, witness testimony, a copy of a will, list of debtors and creditors, names of executors or trustees, names of heirs. They can not only tell you about the ancestor you're currently researching, but lead to other ancestors.

Tennessee State Library and Archives – Huge collection of probate records and deeds from every county in the state dating from the late 18th century

403 7th Avenue North
Nashville, TN 37243
Tel: 615-741-2764
Email: reference.tsla@tn.gov

Tennessee State Library and Archives:
http://www.tn.gov/tsla/Collections.htm

Metro Archives of Nashville and Davidson County – Wills, 1783-1924

Metro Archives
3801 Green Hills Village Drive
Nashville, TN 37215
Phone: 615-862-5880
Email: info@nashvillearchives.org

Metro Archives of Nashville and Davidson County:
http://www.nashvillearchives.org/

The Knox County Archives - Knox County Register of Deeds, Warranty Deed Books, Knox County Probate Records, 1792–1979

East Tennessee History Center
601 S. Gay Street
Knoxville, TN 37902
Phone:(865) 215-8800
Email: archives@knoxlib.org

The Knox County Archives:
http://knoxrooms.sirsi.net/rooms/portal/page/21590_Knox_County_
Archives

Family Search has the following indexes that can be searched online for free:

Tennessee, Probate Court Books, 1795-1927:
https://familysearch.org/search/collection/1909088

Tennessee, Probate Court Files, 1795-1927:
https://familysearch.org/search/collection/1909193

Tennessee, Putnam County Records, 1842-1955:
https://familysearch.org/search/collection/2001083

Tennessee, White County Records, 1809-1975:
https://familysearch.org/search/collection/1989162

Tennessee, Cocke County Records, 1860-1930 :
https://familysearch.org/search/collection/2001053

Tennessee Immigration and Naturalization Records

The naturalization process generated many types of records, including petitions, declarations of intention, and oaths of allegiance. These records can provide family historians with information such as a person's birth date and place of birth, immigration year, marital status, spouse information, occupation, witnesses' names and addresses, and more.

If your ancestor lived in or near a large city, or near a city where U.S. courts convened, you may find naturalization records in the **U.S. District Court** before 1906.

U.S. District Court:
http://www.uscourts.gov/FederalCourts/UnderstandingtheFederalCo urts/DistrictCourts.aspx

For the rural areas of Tennessee, naturalization records may be found with the **County Clerk** in each county. Often the records were mixed in with other court proceedings making them difficult to locate. A few counties kept separate records for naturalization. After 1906, all naturalizations were handled in Federal District Courts.

County Clerk: http://www.tncourts.gov/courts/court-clerks/clerks-list

Tennessee State Library and Archives – Copies of court records for many of the counties in Tennessee. Naturalization records could be in the court minutes for the county court, court of common pleas, circuit court, or chancery court

403 7th Avenue North
Nashville, TN 37243
Tel: 615-741-2764
Email: reference.tsla@tn.gov

Tennessee State Library and Archives:
http://www.tn.gov/tsla/Collections.htm

US National Archives – Immigration records, Naturalization records, Ship's Passenger lists

The National Archives and Records Administration
8601 Adelphi Road
College Park, MD 20740-6001
Tel: 1-866-272-6272; 1-86-NARA-NARAS

US National Archives: http://www.archives.gov/research/guide-fed-records/groups/085.html

Tennessee Native American Records

Tennessee State Library and Archives - Census Roll, 1835, of Cherokee Indians East of the Mississippi, Cherokee Indian Census of 1835 for the States of Georgia, Alabama, and North Carolina, Cherokee Emigration Rolls, 1817-1835, Cherokee Property Evaluation, 1836, Cherokee and Creek Indians. Returns of Property Left in Tennessee and Georgia, 1838, Enrollment Cards for the Five Civilized Tribes, 1898-1914, and a variety of other valuable Native American resources and research guides

403 7th Avenue North
Nashville, TN 37243
Tel: 615-741-2764
Email: reference.tsla@tn.gov

Tennessee State Library and Archives:
http://www.tn.gov/tsla/Collections.htm

Williamson County Public Library - Eastern Cherokee census records

1314 Columbia Ave.
Franklin, TN 37064
Telephone: 615-794-3105
Fax: 615-595-1245

Williamson County Public Library: http://lib.williamson-tn.org/

Access Genealogy – Tennessee Native American census records, tribal histories, and much more

Access Genealogy:
http://www.accessgenealogy.com/native/Tennessee-indian-tribes.htm

U.S. National Archives - information on American Indians who maintained their ties to Federally-recognized Tribes (1830-1970).

U.S. National Archives: http://www.archives.gov/research/native-americans/

Records of the Bureau of Indian Affairs (BIA)

Records of the Bureau of Indian Affairs (BIA): http://www.archives.gov/research/guide-fed-records/groups/075.html

American Indians Records Repository - records dating from the 1700s including trust, education and other historic Indian Affairs records

American Indian Records Repository
Meritex Enterprises
17501 West 98th Street
Lenexa, KS 66219
Phone: 913-888-0601

American Indians Records Repository: http://www.doi.gov/ost/records_mgmt/american-indian-records-repository.cfm

Missing Matriarchs – Resources for Researching Female Tennessee Ancestors

Looking for female ancestors requires an adjustment of how we view traditional records sources. A woman's identity was often under that of her husband, and often individual records for them can be difficult to locate. The following resources are effective in locating female ancestors in Tennessee where traditional records may not reveal them.

Bibliographies

- *Tennessee Women, Past and Present, Wilma Dykeman (Committee for the Humanities, 1977)*
- *Tennessee Families: A Bibliography of Books About Tennessee Families,* Donald M. Hehir (Heritage Books, 1996)
- *Distinctive Women of Tennessee,* James A. Hoobler (Tennessee Historical Association)
- *Shaping of a State: The Legacy of Tennessee Women,* Thura Mack (Cuningson Women's Center, 1995)
- *Quilts of Appalachia: The Mountain Woman and Her Quilt,* Martha Marshall (Tri- City, 1972)

Selected Resources for Tennessee Women's History

Archives of Appalachia, Sherrod Library
East Tennessee State University
Johnson City, TN 37614-0002

Tennessee Collection
Andrew L. Todd Library
Middle Tennessee State University
Murfreesboro, TN 37132

Tennessee Women's Network
403 Seventh Avenue North
Nashville, TN 37243-0312

Common Tennessee Surnames

The following surnames are among the most common in Tennessee and are also being currently researched by other genealogists. If you find your surname here, there is a chance that some research has already been performed on your ancestor.

Agnes, Anderson, Anthony, Armstrong, Askew, Austin, Baggett, Barks, Barrett, Bess, Black, Blum, Bouldin, Bratcher, Brown, Byars, Campbell, Cantrell, Childers, Choate, Cinda, Collier, Cooley, Cooper, Corey, Crawford, Cunningham, Davidson, Deamie, Deberry, Derryberry, Doak, Dorothy, Dresser, Duckett, Durham, Dykes, Elizabeth, Ernest, Estridge, Fay, Ferguson, Forsyth, Friend, Gann, Garner, Garrad, Gray, Green, Hale, Haney, Hawkins, Herendon, Hewitt, Hill, Johnson, Jr, Kimball, King, Lamance, Lancaster, Lankford, Lemmon, Lewis, Lorena, Marcum, Margaret, Marshall, Marx, Mary, Mcguffee, Miller, Morrison, Morton, Neal, Newberry, Nickerson, Norris, Owen, Patty, Pearl, Pelham, Perkins, Pike, Porter, Potter, Pritchard, Randall, Robbins, Russel, Russell, Ryan, Sarah, Seitz, Smartt, Smith, Sr, Stone, Sumner, Tate, Tennpenny, Thorley, Tripp, Turner, Ursala, Vaughn, Wallis, Walters, Watkins, Watson, Webb, Whipple, White, Whitman, Whitmire, Witt

About the Author

Gary L. Morris worked from 2009 to 2014 as a professional researcher for a major player in the genealogy field. After tracing his family lineage back to 1683, he found that genealogy could be an expensive undertaking. As such, has decided to publish these helpful guides to share the valuable free information he has discovered during his career to help others trace their family lineages as inexpensively as possible. An avid genealogist himself, he hopes you will find this guide factual, thorough, helpful, and most of all, effective in helping you to find your family members.

Notes

Notes